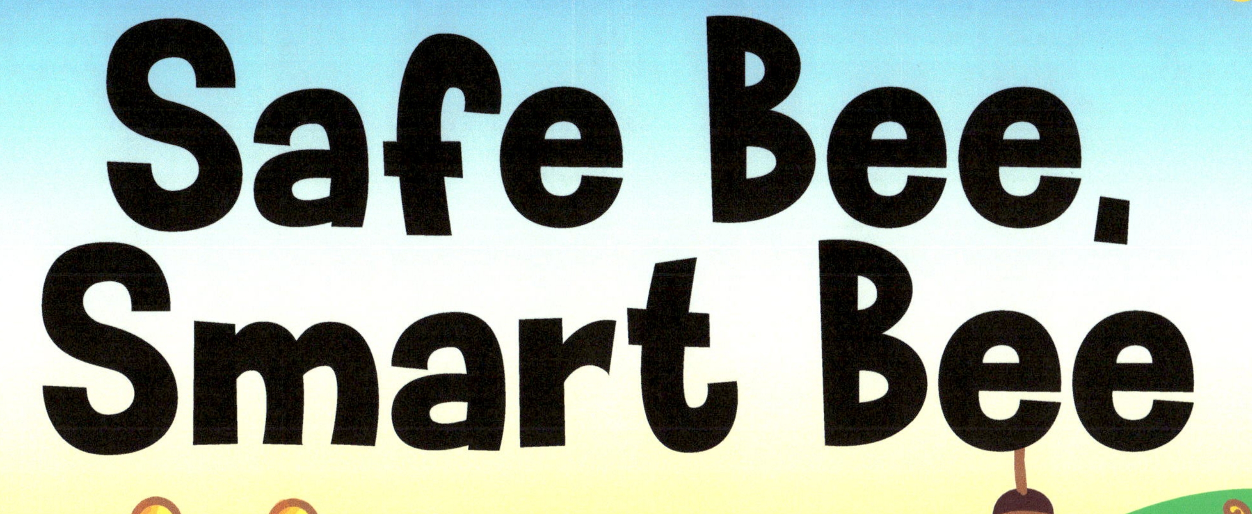

Safe Bee, Smart Bee

By Jennifer Jones

Paperback ISBN:979-8-89614-013-9
Hardcover ISBN:979-8-89614-014-6
For more information, email jenniferjonesbooks@gmail.com

Safe Bee, Smart Bee

A Kid's Book About Staying Safe in Danger's Way

By Jennifer Jones

In a sunny field, where flowers bloom,
The bees fly to and fro.
But when a bear comes sniffing around,
It's time to take it slow.

BZZZ
ZZ

The Queen Bee says, "Don't worry, friends,
We'll handle this just fine.
If danger comes, we'll work as one,
Just follow my every sign."

"When trouble comes, you'll hear my voice,
So listen close and clear.
I'll guide you through with simple steps,
There's nothing here to fear."

First, the Queen Bee locks the hive,
No buzzing out the door.
We stay inside, keep still and quiet,
Until we learn more.

"Stay calm and still, just like I said,
And don't peek out or fly.
We'll stay hidden, safe and sound,
While danger passes by."

STAY STILL

But if the bear is far away,
We'll move when it's alright.
The Queen will lead us out the hive,
And guide us out of sight.

SAFETY
PACKS
SAFETY
PACKS

We fly together, in a line,
No rush, no need to race.
We stick close to the Queen Bee's lead,
And find a safer place.
SAFETY PACKS
SAFETY PACKS

But sometimes staying put's the best,
No need to make a sound.
We'll wait until the coast is clear,
Then safely buzz around.

With doors shut tight and no one seen,
We're hidden safe inside.
We know the Queen's protecting us,
So we just wait and hide.
SAFE

When the bear has gone for good,
The Queen Bee gives a cheer.
"You did so great, you stayed so calm,
You're safe now, never fear!"

So when you're at school and hear the call,
Remember the bees' smart way.
Stay cool, stay still, and listen well,
You'll all be safe today.

The Queen Bee knows what steps to take,
She'll guide you every time.
Just like the bees, you'll work as one,
And everything will be fine.

In every hive, the bees stay safe,
When they all work as a team.
And in your school, you're safe as well—
It's easier than it seems.

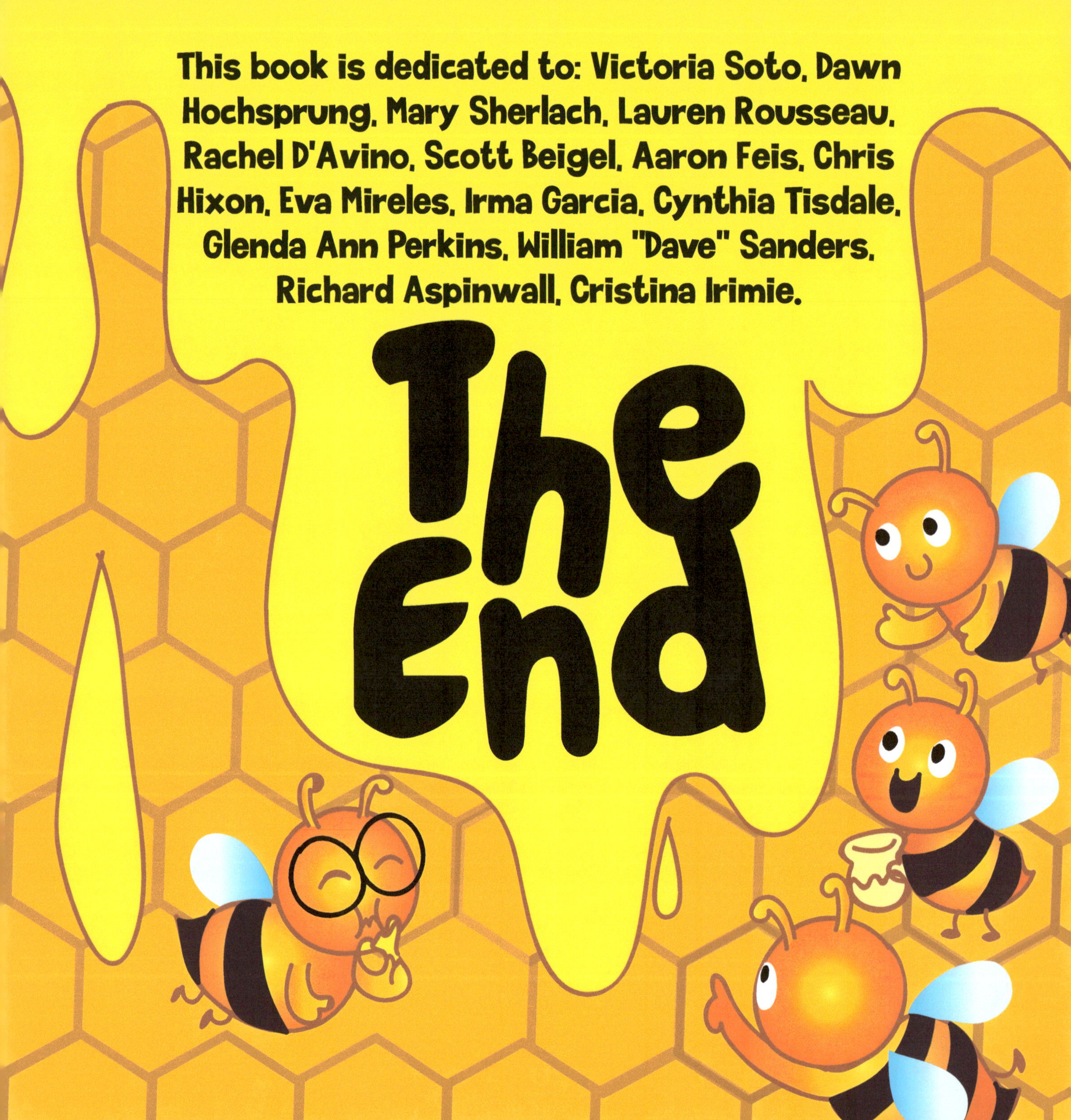

This book is dedicated to: Victoria Soto, Dawn Hochsprung, Mary Sherlach, Lauren Rousseau, Rachel D'Avino, Scott Beigel, Aaron Feis, Chris Hixon, Eva Mireles, Irma Garcia, Cynthia Tisdale, Glenda Ann Perkins, William "Dave" Sanders, Richard Aspinwall, Cristina Irimie.
The End

The goal of this book is to introduce safety steps in a way that's approachable for children of all ages. By engaging with these strategies, children can better understand how to stay safe if they ever face a dangerous situation.

www.ingramcontent.com/pod-product-compliance
Lightning Source LLC
Chambersburg PA
CBHW042031110726
48010CB00008B/295